STORY:
ELIZABETH HUDSON-GOFF AND JONATHA A. BROWN

ILLUSTRATIONS:
GUUS FLOOR, D. MCHARGUE, AND JONATHAN TIMMONS

WORLD ALMANAC® LIBRARY

THERE WAS A TIME NOT LONG AGO WHEN JEWS WERE HUNTED DOWN AND KILLED ALL OVER EUROPE. NO ONE WAS SAFE. PARENTS, GRANDPARENTS, CHILDREN, AND BABIES WERE HERDED TOGETHER LIKE CATTLE. THEY WERE TAKEN TO TERRIFYING PLACES CALLED DEATH CAMPS.

BETWEEN 1933 AND 1945, NAZI GERMANY KILLED UP TO 12 MILLION PEOPLE. MOST WERE MURDERED BECAUSE OF THEIR RELIGION, RACE, OR POLITICAL BELIEFS. SIX MILLION OF THESE PEOPLE WERE JEWS. THIS MASS MURDER OF THE JEWS OF EUROPE IS ONE OF HISTORY'S DARKEST TIMES. IT IS NOW CALLED THE HOLOCAUST.

IN GERMANY AND NATIONS CONTROLLED BY THE NAZIS, THOUSANDS OF FAMILIES TOOK THEIR CHILDREN INTO HIDING TO TRY TO ESCAPE. ANNE FRANK WAS ONE OF THESE CHILDREN.

FOR ALMOST TWO YEARS, ANNE AND HER FAMILY HID IN AN ATTIC IN AMSTERDAM, THE NETHERLANDS. DURING THIS TIME, SHE KEPT A DIARY. SHE SHARED HER SECRET FEARS AND DREAMS IN THIS SMALL, BLANK BOOK. SHE WROTE ABOUT WHAT DAILY LIFE WAS LIKE FOR A YOUNG TEENAGER DURING THE HOLOCAUST.

HER DIARY WAS LATER PUBLISHED. IT IS NOW ONE OF THE MOST WIDELY READ BOOKS IN THE WORLD.

ANNE WAS BORN IN FRANKFURT, GERMANY, ON JUNE 12, 1929. SHE HAD AN OLDER SISTER NAMED MARGOT. HER PARENTS, OTTO AND EDITH, ADORED THEIR TWO CHILDREN.

THE FRANKS WERE JEWISH. MANY OF THEIR FRIENDS WERE CHRISTIAN. THE FRANKS KNEW THEIR CHRISTIAN FRIENDS THOUGHT OF THEM AS A LITTLE "DIFFERENT," ESPECIALLY DURING HOLIDAYS LIKE CHRISTMAS AND HANUKKAH. BUT THESE DIFFERENCES DID NOT GET IN THE WAY OF THEIR FRIENDSHIPS.

THESE HAPPY DAYS WOULD NOT LAST.

BOTH GIRLS HAD MANY FRIENDS GROWING UP. MARGOT WAS KNOWN TO BE SHY AND SWEET. ANNE WAS FUNNY, ACTIVE, AND CURIOUS. HER TEACHERS CALLED HER A "CHATTERBOX." SHE WAS ALSO SMART, WITH STRONG VIEWS ABOUT THE WORLD.

ANNE WANTED TO BE FAMOUS WHEN SHE GREW UP. SHE DREAMED OF BEING A MOVIE STAR OR A WRITER. LIKE MOST KIDS, SHE MADE BIG PLANS FOR HER LIFE. UNLIKE HER NON-JEWISH FRIENDS, HOWEVER, SHE WOULD SOON LEARN HOW LITTLE THE REST OF THE WORLD CARED ABOUT THOSE PLANS—OR HER LIFE.

SHORTLY AFTER ANNE WAS BORN, A WORLDWIDE CRISIS CALLED THE GREAT DEPRESSION BEGAN. PEOPLE COULD NOT AFFORD TO BUY THE THINGS THEY NEEDED, LIKE GROCERIES, FOOD, AND MEDICINE. THE CRISIS HIT GERMANY HARD. MILLIONS OF GERMANS LOST THEIR JOBS. PEOPLE EVERYWHERE LINED UP IN THE STREETS FOR SOUP AND A PIECE OF BREAD. OTTO FRANK LOST MOST OF HIS BUSINESS. THE FRANKS HAD TO MOVE TO A SMALLER HOME.

A TERRIBLE MAN NAMED ADOLF HITLER TOOK ADVANTAGE OF THOSE HARD TIMES FOR HIS OWN DARK PURPOSE. HE LED THE NAZIS, A GROUP THAT PREACHED HATRED TOWARD JEWS AND OTHER ETHNIC GROUPS. HITLER SWORE THAT HE COULD MAKE GERMANY A GREAT COUNTRY AGAIN. WHAT HE REALLY WANTED, THOUGH, WAS TO RULE ALL OF EUROPE.

AT FIRST, NOT MANY PEOPLE LISTENED TO HITLER. AS GERMANY'S PROBLEMS GREW WORSE, HOWEVER, HITLER GAINED ATTENTION. HE STAGED GRAND PARADES AND GAVE WILD SPEECHES. HE EXCITED CROWDS WITH HIS PROMISES TO DESTROY THE ENEMIES OF GERMANY.

HITLER BELIEVED PEOPLE SHOULD BE JUDGED ON THE BASIS OF THEIR RACE. HE THOUGHT THE ONLY "PURE" RACE WAS THE "ARYAN" RACE. HE DESCRIBED ARYANS AS PEOPLE WITH FAIR SKIN AND HAIR WHO ORIGINALLY CAME FROM NORTHERN EUROPE. HE SAID THAT ONLY ARYANS SHOULD LIVE IN GERMANY.

RACE BECAME HITLER'S EXCUSE TO TARGET MANY GROUPS AS ENEMIES OF GERMANY. BUT HE SINGLED OUT ONE GROUP FOR ESPECIALLY BAD TREATMENT—THE JEWS. OVER AND OVER, HITLER CALLED JEWS "INFERIOR" AND "EVIL." HE WARNED THAT PEOPLE LIKE ANNE AND HER FAMILY WANTED TO TAKE OVER GERMANY, THEN THE WORLD. HE USED VIOLENCE AND EVEN MASS MURDER TO ACHIEVE HIS GOAL—TO MAKE GERMANY JUDENREIN, OR FREE OF JEWS.

IN JANUARY 1933, HITLER WAS ELECTED TO LEAD GERMANY. HE GOT TO WORK QUICKLY. HE THREW OUT MANY OF GERMANY'S LAWS AND NAMED HIMSELF DICTATOR. AS DICTATOR, HITLER COULD DO ANYTHING HE WANTED TO DO. HE HAD THE NEWSPAPERS PRINT HATE-FILLED ARTICLES ABOUT JEWS. HIS RADIO BROADCASTS SPOKE OUT AGAINST THE JEWS.

HITLER ALSO FORMED A SPECIAL POLICE FORCE CALLED THE GESTAPO. THEY USED TERROR TO CONTROL THE GERMAN PEOPLE.

THE FRANKS NO LONGER FELT SAFE IN GERMANY. IN 1933, THE FAMILY MOVED TO AMSTERDAM, IN THE NETHERLANDS. THERE, MARGOT AND FOUR-YEAR-OLD ANNE LEARNED TO SPEAK DUTCH. THEY MADE FRIENDS EASILY.

OTTO WAS OFTEN AWAY FROM HOME BECAUSE OF HIS JOB, BUT THE FAMILY ENJOYED MANY GOOD TIMES. THEY TRAVELED AND SAW FILMS. ANNE WAS OFTEN SICK AS A YOUNG CHILD BUT REMAINED OUTGOING AND CHEERFUL. SHE EVEN GOT IN TROUBLE AT SCHOOL FOR TALKING SO MUCH!

MEANWHILE, THE NAZIS WERE GROWING STRONGER. BY 1938, MOST JEWS IN GERMANY HAD LOST ALL OF THEIR RIGHTS. THE GESTAPO AND OTHERS BEAT THEM FOR BREAKING "LAWS" THAT DID NOT EXIST. JEWISH BUSINESSES WERE CLOSED DOWN, AND JEWISH BOOKS BURNED. JEWISH PLACES OF WORSHIP WENT UP IN FLAMES AS WELL. PEOPLE WHO WERE ARRESTED WERE OFTEN NEVER SEEN AGAIN. THE FRANKS THOUGHT THEY HAD MOVED JUST IN TIME.

BUT IN REALITY, TIME WAS RUNNING OUT FOR THE JEWS ALL OVER EUROPE.

IN JANUARY 1941, THE TERROR BEGAN IN A SIMPLE, CHILLING WAY. THE NAZIS MADE ALL JEWS IN THE NETHERLANDS REGISTER WITH THE NEW GOVERNMENT. NOW, THE NAZIS HAD A WAY TO TRACK DOWN EVERY JEW IN THE COUNTRY.

ANNE REALIZED THAT LIFE WAS CHANGING FOR HER AND HER FAMILY. NOTHING MADE SENSE ANYMORE. ONE DAY, SHE WAS TOLD SHE COULD NO LONGER RIDE HER BIKE. ANOTHER DAY, SHE WAS WARNED NEVER TO LEAVE THE HOUSE AT NIGHT. JEWS COULD NOT SWIM IN PUBLIC POOLS OR GO TO THE MOVIES.

EVERY MORNING, ANNE'S HEART BEAT WITH FEAR. WHAT NEW RULE HAD BEEN MADE TODAY TO HURT THE JEWS? WHAT WOULD HAPPEN IF SHE BROKE A RULE?

ANNE AND MARGOT WERE SENT TO A JEWISH SCHOOL BECAUSE JEWISH CHILDREN COULD NOT "MIX" WITH CHRISTIANS ANYMORE. STILL, ANNE SAW HER FRIENDS AND TRIED TO LIVE AS NORMAL A LIFE AS POSSIBLE. MAYBE, SHE THOUGHT, THINGS WOULD START TO GET BETTER. MAYBE THE WAR WOULD END SOON.

ONE DAY, EDITH FRANK SHOWED HER GIRLS A LARGE YELLOW STAR. SHE SAID THAT ALL JEWS NOW HAD TO WEAR THIS STAR ON ALL OF THEIR CLOTHES. SOLDIERS MIGHT BEAT THEM OR TAKE THEM AWAY IF THEY DID NOT WEAR IT.

WHEN ANNE WENT OUT, SOME PEOPLE POINTED AT HER AND CALLED HER NAMES LIKE "DIRTY JEW." THEY WANTED HER TO FEEL BAD AND DIFFERENT.

AT ABOUT THE SAME TIME, HITLER WAS MAKING HIS OWN PLANS TO MURDER EVERY JEW IN EUROPE!

FOR ANNE'S THIRTEENTH BIRTHDAY, SHE WAS GIVEN A SMALL DIARY. THE DIARY WAS HER FAVORITE GIFT. ANNE TALKED A LOT, BUT SHE WAS ALSO VERY PRIVATE. FOR THE REST OF HER SHORT LIFE, THIS BOOK WOULD BE HER CLOSEST FRIEND.

"I HOPE I WILL BE ABLE TO CONFIDE EVERYTHING TO YOU, AS I HAVE NEVER BEEN ABLE TO CONFIDE IN ANYONE, AND I HOPE YOU WILL BE A GREAT SOURCE OF COMFORT AND SUPPORT." ANNE'S FIRST DIARY ENTRY, JUNE 12, 1942

"THIS IS NOT THE END. IT IS NOT EVEN THE BEGINNING OF THE END. BUT IT IS, PERHAPS, THE END OF THE BEGINNING."
ANNE FRANK, NOVEMBER 9, 1942

ONE DAY, ANNE'S FATHER TOLD HER SHOCKING NEWS. HE SAID THAT THE FAMILY WOULD NEED TO MOVE FROM THEIR HOUSE AND GO INTO HIDING. HE SAID THAT THE FAMILY WAS NO LONGER SAFE FROM THE NAZIS. HE TOLD ANNE NOT TO WORRY, BUT SHE FELT VERY SCARED. WHERE WOULD THEY GO? WAS ANY PLACE SAFE?

ON JULY 5, 1942, THE FRANKS RECEIVED AWFUL NEWS. THE NAZIS WERE ORDERING SIXTEEN-YEAR-OLD MARGOT TO GO TO A "LABOR CAMP." ANNE BEGAN TO CRY. SHE HAD NEVER SEEN HER PARENTS SO AFRAID. ANNE WAS TOLD TO PACK HER MOST IMPORTANT THINGS IN A SCHOOLBAG AND HURRY. THE FIRST ITEM ANNE PUT IN WAS HER DIARY.

ON A RAINY DAY, JULY 9, 1942, THE FRANKS LEFT THEIR HOME FOR THE LAST TIME. ANNE WROTE, "THE FOUR OF US WERE DRESSED IN SO MANY LAYERS OF CLOTHES IT LOOKED AS IF WE WERE GOING OFF TO SPEND THE NIGHT IN A REFRIGERATOR." ALTHOUGH THE FAMILY HAD MANAGED TO STAY TOGETHER, ANNE'S HEART BROKE. SHE HAD TO LEAVE HER BELOVED CAT, MOOTJE, BEHIND.

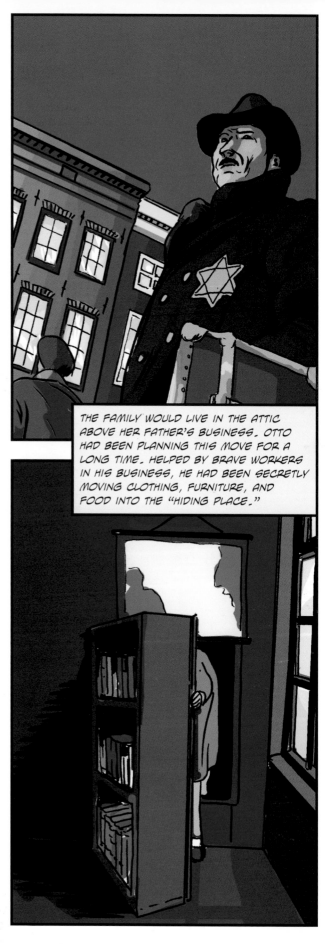

THE FAMILY WOULD LIVE IN THE ATTIC ABOVE HER FATHER'S BUSINESS. OTTO HAD BEEN PLANNING THIS MOVE FOR A LONG TIME. HELPED BY BRAVE WORKERS IN HIS BUSINESS, HE HAD BEEN SECRETLY MOVING CLOTHING, FURNITURE, AND FOOD INTO THE "HIDING PLACE."

AT FIRST, ANNE SAW HER NEW LIFE AS AN ADVENTURE. SHE CALLED THEIR NEW HOME THE "SECRET ANNEX." OTTO HAD REMEMBERED TO BRING ANNE'S MOVIE STAR POSTERS. SHE HAPPILY HUNG THEM IN HER ROOM.

THE ATTIC WAS QUITE LARGE. THE FRANKS SHARED THE SPACE WITH ANOTHER JEWISH FAMILY, THE VAN PELS. THEY HAD A SIXTEEN-YEAR-OLD SON NAMED PETER. LATER, A JEWISH DENTIST JOINED THE GROUP AND SHARED A ROOM WITH ANNE. IN ALL, EIGHT PEOPLE LIVED IN THE HIDING PLACE.

IT WAS HARD FOR ANNE TO GET USED TO THIS NEW LIFE. SHE COULD NOT GO OUTSIDE. THE WINDOWS WERE COVERED AND COULD NEVER BE OPENED. SHE FELT ANNOYED AT TIMES AND OFTEN ARGUED WITH THE ADULTS.

BUT SHE ALSO WROTE ABOUT HOW LUCKY SHE AND HER FAMILY WERE TO BE IN HIDING. SHE WROTE, "TERRIBLE THINGS ARE HAPPENING OUTSIDE . . . CHILDREN COME HOME FROM SCHOOL TO FIND THAT THEIR PARENTS HAVE DISAPPEARED."

THEIR HELPERS FROM BELOW BROUGHT THEM FOOD AND OTHER SUPPLIES. THE HIDING PLACE WAS KEPT SECRET FROM THE REST OF THE WORKERS. THERE WAS ALWAYS A CHANCE THAT SOMEONE WOULD TELL THE POLICE.

DAYS IN THE ATTIC WERE MUCH THE SAME. ANNE WOKE EARLY AND HELPED WITH CHORES. THEN, SHE STUDIED, WROTE IN HER DIARY, AND HELPED WITH DINNER. SHE WROTE, "WHO WOULD HAVE GUESSED THREE MONTHS AGO THAT QUICKSILVER ANNE WOULD HAVE TO SIT SO QUIETLY FOR HOURS ON END, AND WHAT'S MORE, THAT SHE COULD?"

NIGHTS WERE SCARY. THE AIR WAS FILLED WITH TERRIFYING SOUNDS OF PLANES, BOMBS, AND GUNS.

EVEN WORSE, ANNE WROTE, WERE THE QUIET NIGHTS. ANNE IMAGINED THAT SHE HEARD FOOTSTEPS COMING TOWARD THE SECRET DOOR. SHE IMAGINED COLD-EYED NAZIS BURSTING INTO THE ROOM. ONE NIGHT, THIEVES BROKE INTO THE BUILDING AND STOLE SOME MONEY. EVERYONE WAS SURE THE NOISES BELOW WERE FROM THE NAZIS. WHAT RELIEF TO FIND THE NOISE WAS ONLY FROM ROBBERS!

"SO FAR YOU TRULY HAVE BEEN A GREAT SOURCE OF COMFORT TO ME. . . . . NOW I CAN HARDLY WAIT FOR THOSE MOMENTS WHEN I'M ABLE TO WRITE IN YOU. . . . . OH, I'M SO GLAD I BROUGHT YOU ALONG!" SEPTEMBER 28, 1942

DURING THE FRANKS' HIDING, ANNE FILLED HER DIARY WITH HER THOUGHTS AND DREAMS. SHE WROTE ABOUT WAR. SHE WROTE, "THERE'S A DESTRUCTIVE URGE IN PEOPLE, THE URGE TO RAGE, MURDER, AND KILL."

ANNE KNEW JEWS WERE BEING KILLED ALL AROUND HER. ANNE HEARD ABOUT THE DEATH CAMPS ON THE FAMILY'S SECRET RADIO. FROM WITHIN HER TINY ATTIC SHE WROTE, "THESE POOR PEOPLE ARE BEING SHIPPED OFF TO FILTHY SLAUGHTERHOUSES LIKE A HERD OF SICK AND NEGLECTED CATTLE. BUT I'LL SAY NO MORE ON THE SUBJECT. MY OWN THOUGHTS GIVE ME NIGHTMARES!"

BUT MANY OF HER ENTRIES WERE ABOUT THE NORMAL
FEELINGS OF A GROWING TEENAGER. SHE WROTE ABOUT
HER CHANGING BODY AND FEELINGS. SOMETIMES SHE
GOT MAD AT HER PARENTS, ESPECIALLY HER MOTHER.
SHE DEVELOPED A BIG CRUSH ON PETER.

ANNE ALWAYS KEPT UP HOPE
THAT THE WAR WOULD SOON
END. SHE MADE PLANS FOR
WHAT SHE WOULD WEAR AND
WHAT SHE WOULD EAT WHEN
THE FAMILY WAS FREE. AS SHE
GREW, SHE THOUGHT ABOUT
HATRED. SHE WONDERED HOW
PEOPLE COULD TURN AGAINST
A WHOLE GROUP OF PEOPLE.

THE CONSTANT FEAR, CRAMPED CONDITIONS, AND BAD FOOD WERE HARD TO BEAR. ANNE WROTE,
"I'VE ASKED MYSELF AGAIN AND AGAIN WHETHER IT WOULDN'T HAVE BEEN BETTER IF WE HADN'T
GONE INTO HIDING, IF WE WERE DEAD NOW AND DIDN'T HAVE TO GO THROUGH THIS MISERY . . .
BUT WE SHRINK FROM THIS THOUGHT. WE STILL LOVE LIFE, WE HAVEN'T YET FORGOTTEN THE VOICE
OF NATURE, AND WE KEEP HOPING, HOPING FOR . . . EVERYTHING."

"I KEEP TRYING TO FIND A WAY TO BECOME WHAT I'D LIKE TO BE AND WHAT I COULD BE . . . IF ONLY THERE WERE NO OTHER PEOPLE IN THE WORLD." AUGUST 1, 1944, ANNE FRANK'S LAST DIARY ENTRY.

ON AUGUST 4, 1944, THE FAMILY'S WORST FEARS CAME TRUE. A GERMAN POLICEMAN AND FOUR DUTCH NAZIS BURST INTO THE ATTIC. SOMEONE HAD TIPPED OFF THE NAZIS ABOUT THEIR HIDING PLACE. EIGHT SCARED PEOPLE WERE ORDERED DOWN THE STAIRS. ANNE WAS NUMB WITH FEAR.

THE FRANKS WERE KEPT IN A "HOLDING" CAMP FOR NEARLY A MONTH. THEN, THE FRANK FAMILY AND OVER 1,000 OTHER PEOPLE WERE LOADED ONTO CATTLE CARS ON TRAINS. THE TRAIN RIDE LASTED THREE NIGHTS AND TWO DAYS. IT WAS SO CROWDED THAT ANNE AND MARGOT SLEPT LEANING AGAINST THEIR PARENTS. THERE WAS NO FOOD OR WATER. THE ONE TOILET SPILLED ALL OVER THE FLOOR. PEOPLE DIED NEXT TO ANNE ON THE WAY.

THE ONLY THING ANNE HAD LEFT WAS HER FAMILY. SHE WAS TOO NUMB WITH FEAR TO THINK ABOUT WHAT LAY AHEAD. THIS WAS REALLY HAPPENING. SHE WAS GOING TO DIE.

THE TRAIN STOPPED AT AUSCHWITZ, A DEATH CAMP IN POLAND. IT WAS DARK. PEOPLE WERE SHOUTING AND CRYING. ANNE FELL OUT OF THE TRAIN AND WAS PULLED AND PUSHED. DOGS SNAPPED ALL AROUND HER. GUARDS BEAT PEOPLE WITH STICKS. HUGE CHIMNEYS BURNED WITH BRIGHT FLAMES. ANN FELT THAT SHE MIGHT BE IN HELL.

THE MEN AND WOMEN WERE SEPARATED INTO TWO LINES. ANNE TRIED TO CLING TO HER ADORED FATHER, BUT SHE WAS PULLED AWAY. HE GAVE ONE LAST LOOK AT HIS BELOVED DAUGHTERS AND HE WAS GONE.

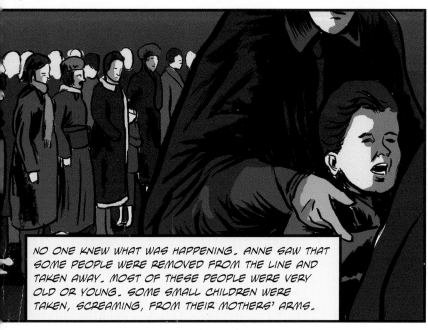

NO ONE KNEW WHAT WAS HAPPENING. ANNE SAW THAT SOME PEOPLE WERE REMOVED FROM THE LINE AND TAKEN AWAY. MOST OF THESE PEOPLE WERE VERY OLD OR YOUNG. SOME SMALL CHILDREN WERE TAKEN, SCREAMING, FROM THEIR MOTHERS' ARMS.

THE NAZIS SHOVED THESE PEOPLE INTO "SHOWERS." BUT THESE "SHOWERS" WERE REALLY DEADLY GAS CHAMBERS

ONLY MONTHS BEFORE, ANNE WAS IN THE LOVING, SAFE CARE OF HER FAMILY. NOW, SHE WAS IN THE HANDS OF MONSTERS. SHE AND THE OTHER WOMEN WERE "PROCESSED." A NUMBER WAS TATTOOED INTO HER ARM. SHE WAS SHAVED FROM HEAD TO FOOT—HER BEAUTIFUL, DARK HAIR GONE. SHE WAS MADE TO STRIP NAKED AND SPRAYED WITH COLD WATER. THEN SHE HAD TO JUMP INTO A HARSH, GERM-KILLING SOLUTION.

ANNE, MARGOT, AND EDITH WERE TAKEN TO A PART OF THE CAMP CALLED BIRKENAU. EVERY DAY, WOMEN AROUND HER WERE HERDED TO THE GAS CHAMBERS. THEIR BODIES WERE PUT INTO LARGE OVENS. THE SMELL OF BURNING FLESH WAS IN THE AIR ALL THE TIME. THE WOMEN WERE HUNGRY AND COLD. NOTHING FELT REAL. MANY WOMEN DIED FROM DISEASE. OTHERS FOUGHT EACH OTHER FOR THE TINY BIT OF FOOD HANDED OUT EACH DAY.

AFTER TWO MONTHS IN BIRKENAU, SOLDIERS TOOK ANNE AND MARGOT AWAY FROM THEIR MOTHER. THEY ONLY HAD EACH OTHER, NOW.

ANNE AND MARGOT WERE SENT TO ANOTHER DEATH CAMP IN GERMANY, CALLED BERGEN-BELSEN. HERE, THEY LIVED INSIDE A CROWDED TENT. THE TENT STOOD ON WET CLAY. THERE WAS NO RUNNING WATER OR ELECTRICITY. IT WAS COLD ALL THE TIME. STARVING AND ILL, ANNE LOST ALL HOPE. SHE FELT DEAD INSIDE FROM THE HORRIBLE THINGS SHE HAD SEEN.

THE TENT FELL OVER IN A STORM. THERE WAS NO SHELTER FROM THE COLD OR RAIN FOR DAYS. PEOPLE BEGAN TO DIE EVERY DAY FROM HUNGER AND ILLNESS. WHEN PEOPLE DIED, THEY WERE THROWN OUTSIDE. OTHERS COLLECTED THEIR CLOTHES TO BURN AS FUEL.

IN FEBRUARY 1945, ANNE'S OLD FRIEND HANNELI FOUND OUT THAT ANNE'S TENT WAS VERY NEAR HERS. THEY MET. ONLY A FEW STRANDS OF BARBED WIRE SEPARATED THE TWO.

HANNELI WAS SHOCKED. ANNE WAS VERY THIN AND HAD LOST MOST OF HER HAIR. HER EYES SEEMED DEAD.

WE DON'T HAVE ANYTHING AT ALL TO EAT HERE . . . AND WE ARE COLD; WE DON'T HAVE ANY CLOTHES AND I'VE GOTTEN VERY THIN AND THEY SHAVED MY HAIR.

I DON'T HAVE ANY PARENTS ANYMORE.

IN MARCH 1945, ANNE DIED. MARGOT HAD DIED ONLY DAYS BEFORE. THEY DIED FROM A DISEASE CALLED TYPHUS. NO ONE SAW WHAT HAPPENED TO THEIR BODIES. THEY WERE PROBABLY THROWN INTO A HUGE HOLE WITH THOUSANDS OF OTHER BODIES.

ALL OF THESE BODIES WERE ONCE PEOPLE LIKE ANNE. THESE PEOPLE HAD HOPES AND DREAMS AND FAMILIES THEY LOVED. SO MANY FUTURES WERE LOST IN THOSE TERRIBLE MASS GRAVES.

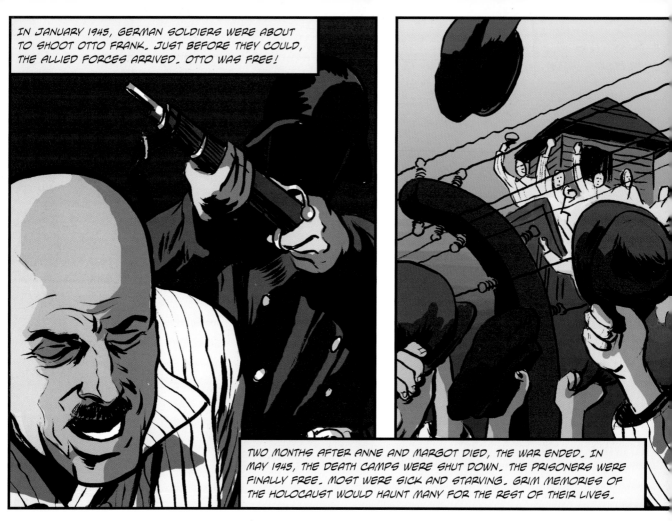

IN JANUARY 1945, GERMAN SOLDIERS WERE ABOUT TO SHOOT OTTO FRANK. JUST BEFORE THEY COULD, THE ALLIED FORCES ARRIVED. OTTO WAS FREE!

TWO MONTHS AFTER ANNE AND MARGOT DIED, THE WAR ENDED. IN MAY 1945, THE DEATH CAMPS WERE SHUT DOWN. THE PRISONERS WERE FINALLY FREE. MOST WERE SICK AND STARVING. GRIM MEMORIES OF THE HOLOCAUST WOULD HAUNT MANY FOR THE REST OF THEIR LIVES.

OTTO SLOWLY MADE THE TRIP BACK TO AMSTERDAM. WHILE HEADING HOME, HE LEARNED THAT EDITH HAD DIED IN AUSCHWITZ. SOON AFTER, HE FOUND OUT THAT ANNE AND MARGOT WERE ALSO DEAD. DEEP SADNESS FILLED HIM.

"AFTER THE WAR I'D LIKE TO PUBLISH A BOOK CALLED THE SECRET ANNEX. IT REMAINS TO BE SEEN WHETHER I'LL SUCCEED, BUT MY DIARY CAN SERVE AS THE BASIS." —MAY 11, 1944

ANNE'S DIARY ALSO MADE IT THROUGH THE WAR. A FRIEND OF THE FAMILY'S HAD HIDDEN IT WHEN ANNE WAS ARRESTED.

OTTO FRANK SPENT MANY HOURS WITH ANNE'S DIARY. HE PRIZED EVERY WORD. FRIENDS HELPED HIM GET THE DIARY PUBLISHED.

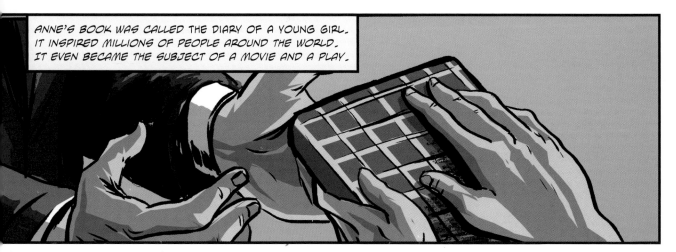

ANNE'S BOOK WAS CALLED THE DIARY OF A YOUNG GIRL. IT INSPIRED MILLIONS OF PEOPLE AROUND THE WORLD. IT EVEN BECAME THE SUBJECT OF A MOVIE AND A PLAY.

OVER HALF THE JEWISH POPULATION IN EUROPE DIED IN THE HOLOCAUST. ALTHOUGH THE NAZIS WERE DETERMINED TO KILL OFF ALL THE JEWS, THEY ALSO KILLED OTHER PEOPLE. THESE PEOPLE HAD DIFFERENT RELIGIONS. THEY CAME FROM DIFFERENT NATIONS AND ETHNIC BACKGROUNDS. THEY THOUGHT ABOUT LIFE DIFFERENTLY THAN THE NAZIS DID. THESE PEOPLE'S BACKGROUNDS AND THEIR BELIEFS MADE THE NAZIS FEEL THEY MUST BE DESTROYED.

AUSCHWITZ

BIRKENAU

BERGEN-BELSEN

ANNE FRANK WAS SMART AND BRAVE. SHE DARED TO DREAM OF A FUTURE THAT FOR HER WOULD NEVER BE. SHE SPOKE FOR MILLIONS OF OTHERS WHOSE LIVES WERE ALSO CUT SHORT.

BECAUSE OF ANNE FRANK, WE BETTER UNDERSTAND THE TERRIBLE THINGS THAT HATRED CAN DO. THROUGH HER WORDS, HOWEVER, WE ALSO UNDERSTAND THE GOODNESS THAT LIES IN THE HEARTS OF MANY. ANNE'S WRITING HAS MOVED PEOPLE TO WORK HARDER FOR PEACE. WITH HER DIARY, ANNE HAS GIVEN A GREAT GIFT TO THE WORLD. THROUGH THE IMPACT OF HER WORDS ON MILLIONS OF PEOPLE, HER DREAMS OF GREATNESS HAVE COME TRUE.

"HOW WONDERFUL IT IS THAT NO ONE HAS TO WAIT, BUT CAN START RIGHT NOW TO GRADUALLY CHANGE THE WORLD!" ANNE FRANK

MORE BOOKS TO READ

Anne Frank (*Trailblazers of the Modern World* series). Jonatha A. Brown
 (World Almanac Library)

Anne Frank. Rachel S. Epstein (Scholastic Library)

Anne Frank: Hope in the Shadows of the Holocaust. Spring Hermann.
 (Enslow Publishers, Incorporated)

Anne Frank: Life in Hiding. Johanna Hurwitz. (HarperCollins Publishers)

Anne Frank and Me. Cherie Bennett, Jeff Gottesfeld.
 (Penguin Putnam Books for Young Readers)

Memories of Anne Frank: reflections of a childhood friend. Alison Leslie Gold (Scholastic)

WEB SITES

The Anne Frank Center
www.annefrank.com/2_students_faqs.htm

Anne Frank: Lessons in Human Rights and Dignity
www.surfnetkids.com/annefrank.htm

Anne Frank, stories, background, activities and more
www.annefrank.org/content.asp?pid=2&lid=2&flashid=2

Survivor, Hero, Anne Frank
myhero.com/myhero/hero.asp

Please visit our web site at: www.worldalmanaclibrary.com
For a free color catalog describing World Almanac® Library's
list of high-quality books and multimedia programs,
call 1-800-848-2928 (USA) or 1-800-387-3178 (Canada).
World Almanac® Library's fax: (414) 332-3567.

Library of Congress Cataloging-in-Publication Data

Hudson-Goff, Elizabeth.
 Anne Frank / Elizabeth Hudson-Goff and Jonatha A. Brown.
  p. cm. — (Graphic biographies)
 Includes bibliographical references.
 ISBN 0-8368-6196-5 (lib. bdg.)
 ISBN 0-8368-6248-1 (softcover)
 1. Frank, Anne, 1929-1945—Juvenile literature. 2. Jewish children in
the Holocaust—Netherlands—Amsterdam--Biography—Juvenile literature.
3. Jews—Netherlands—Amsterdam—Biography—Juvenile literature.
4. Holocaust, Jewish (1939-1945)—Netherlands—Amsterdam—Juvenile
literature. 5. Jewish girls—Netherlands—Amsterdam—Biography—Juvenile
literature. 6. Amsterdam (Netherlands)—Biography—Juvenile literature.
I. Brown, Jonatha A. II. Title. III. Series.
DS135.N6F733433 2006
940.53'18'092—dc22   2005027722

First published in 2006 by
World Almanac® Library
A Member of the WRC Media Family of Companies
330 West Olive Street, Suite 100
Milwaukee, WI 53212 USA

Copyright © 2006 by World Almanac® Library.

Produced by Design Press, a division of the
Savannah College of Art and Design
Design: Janice Shay and Maria Angela Rojas
Editing: Kerri O'Hern and Elizabeth Hudson-Goff
Illustration: Pencils by Guus Floor, inks by D. McHargue,
 color by Jonathan Timmons
World Almanac® Library editorial direction: Mark Sachner
 and Valerie J. Weber
World Almanac® Library art direction: Tammy West

Printed in the United States of America

1 2 3 4 5 6 7 8 9 10 09 08 07 06